Say it With a Poem

Original poems

By Christine M Hannon

Dedication

I would like to thank my friend and editor Jo-Anne Ballarano for all of her time and patience editing these poems for me. My husband Ron, our children and grandchildren for letting me share the poems I wrote about them. I love you all.

Table of Contents

Family Ties

When we were little children,
Everything to us was free,
Nothing had a price to it,
And we wanted all we'd see.

We took so much for granted,
Things that were always there,
The change in Daddy's pocket,
The food the love, the care.

Brothers, sisters, Mom and Dad,
Truly a family make.
Not always is there peace and joy,
Not always give and take.

But as the time does pass us,
And adults we all can be,
Nothing can be taken for granted,
And we find not much is free.

But there is something that we carry,
For each other deep inside,
Something that keeps us caring,
And we call it 'Family Ties'.

Last Goodbye

My friend, this is my last goodbye,
I find the words so hard to say,
I know I really should not cry,
But part of me would like to stay.

A new life is waiting as we go,
And we'll change because of this,
But your friendship will have marked us,
So you I'll truly miss.

My tears are not for sadness,
For you've been a joy to know,
Yet it's hard to say this,
My friend, it's time I go.

Let Me

Let me say it one more time,
Let me prove that you are mine,
Let me hold you, oh so tight,
This time let me do it right.

My world is empty without you,
I really don't know what to do,
The hurt I feel is ever strong,
Oh my darling what went wrong?

Why do I make you turn away?
Is it the things I do not say?
Can't you see my heart is yours?
To you, my life's an open door.

Ask of me and it is done,
To me you are the only one,
I'll love you till the day I die,
But now you're gone and I don't know why.

Baby, baby come back to me,
Give again your love so free,
Baby, baby can't you see,
How deeply you are hurting me.

Fear

Fear! It grips you with its icy claws,
And tears your guts apart,
It makes you break into a sweat,
And causes tears to start.

It makes your body shiver,
And causes nerves to fray,
You lose the right perspective,
Of life in a normal way.

The drawn and tired lines,
That mars your handsome face,
It kills the smile in your eyes,
And sadness takes its place.

But now the nightmares over,
And life you'll start anew,
You've been allowed a second chance,
To do what you like to do.

This summer was a loss to us,
The months just passed us by,
But every seconds precious,
Because you will not die.

If for a second we forget,
How close your family grew,
We surely will soon remember,
When we say the words "I love you".

Close the Door

Close the door on your way out,
Don't come back no more,
I don't need you hanging 'round,
And please don't slam the door.

I packed your bags with all your things,
And returned the ring you gave me,
I could hardly see through my teary eyes,
As you tried to beg, forgive me.

I no longer have a vision,
Of what I thought you were,
I see you as a cheating man,
Now get out and close the door!

Seasons

Those lazy days, those hazy days,
Just before the spring,
Those blowy days and chilly days,
When you don't hear birds that sing.

It's on those days, those dreary days,
When you would like to stay in bed,
Just to dream away the hours,
With covers o'er your head.

Those days are last of winter,
T'was a time of joy and fun,
A time of snowy wonder,
But now those days are done.

I know I am discouraged,
I know that I am blue,
I know I'm not the only one,
Because you feel it too.

And then you'll see a difference,
In the people that you meet,
And it surely won't be long now'
We'll complain about the heat.

Loving You Is

Loving you is
Never being lonely,

Loving you is
Sharing plans and dreams,

Loving you is
Having your children,

Loving you is
Sometimes crying,

Loving you is
Being proud,

Loving you is
Experiencing new things,

Loving you is
Wanting it to never end,

Loving you is
What I do best.

Loving you is
In return for you loving me.

My Man

Close your eyes my darling,
Tell me what you see,
Is your mind upon another?
Or are your thoughts of me.

To hear your voice is heaven,
An angel from above,
I know only in my dreams,
Can we really be in love.

A kiss that causes shivers,
To tingle down my spine,
The warmness of your body,
So very close to mine.

I savor every second,
That you can give to me,
No better gift can I receive,
Than time you're giving free.

My eyes must surely tell you,
The thing my lips daren't say,
Words that are forbidden,
I must show another ways.

My man, my precious darling,
So very strong, but sweet,
The way you're oh so gentle,
Each and every time we meet.

To caress your neck and shoulders,
One could almost hear you purr,
I see the tension on your face,
And you hardly even stir.

If you could have three wishes,
What would those wishes be?
Would I ever be so lucky?
That one would be for me.

Very special records,
I sit and listen to,
Recall those precious memories,
They hold for me and you.

If you should ever leave me,
I know I'd surely cry,
I'd never ever be the same,
'Cause part of me would die.

Making love's so simple,
So beautiful, so grand,
When the one I share it with,
Is you my special man.

Misunderstanding

Isn't he so handsome?
See him standing there,
Eyes of deepest blue,
Sun spun golden hair.

He looks my way and smiles,
I act so sweet and shy,
Can he see that I'm blushing?
Or see the twinkle in my eye?

As he comes much closer,
My heart does pound aloud,
He must like me just a little,
With him I'd be so proud.

And soon he'll be much closer,
He'll be right by my side.
But he only walked right by me,
I wish that I could hide.

She's standing there, just waiting,
With her arms stretched wide apart,
A smile on her ruby lips,
And me with a broken heart.

LIES

Lies! Lies! Lies!
You know that I believed you,
No matter what you said,
You led me on so often,
Your lies went to my head.

You made me think you liked me,
A silly game that you have played,
Made me do things for you,
Lose friends that I have made.

But now I am much smarter,
A lesson I have learned,
You will find that you will suffer,
For now, the tables turned.

My heart will heal, but slowly,
And that will all take time,
But now your lies won't hurt me,
You will suffer for your crime.

Now your lies can't help you,
Your friends will walk away,
Your life will be so lonely,
For the heart you broke today.

Why so Sad

Honey, what is the matter?
You seem so sad these days,
You are so very quiet,
You've changed in many ways.

You've never got a smile
When you come through the door,
You've always talked about your day,
But don't ever do that anymore.

I know it is not fair to you,
That I've been sick in bed,
And you have the extra things to do,
Seeing all is done and kids are fed.

You never complain about it,
Or holler or yell or scream,
Or curse or swear or remind me,
I'm not being part of this team.

I wouldn't blame you for a moment,
If you said, "why should I come home today?
I need more time to myself,
I need some time for play."

Please don't ever let it happen,
You feel I'm a burden to you,
Honey, please do tell me,
If you ever feel it's true.

I Wish That God Would Wait

I will beg you not to leave us,
I will plead with you to stay,
I will cry cause it's not fair,
God moves in a mysterious way.

Why you? I do not understand.
His ways aren't clear to me,
How could He take the best there is,
It simply cannot be.

I love you for your goodness,
For your cheerfulness and care,
And when I need assurance,
You were always there.

I hope I said the right things,
To let you know you're great,
How much I really love you,
And I wish that God would wait.

Come Be With Me

Come be with me,
Come share my life,
Be my man,
I'll be your wife,
Come be with me.

Come share my dreams,
I have for two,
I want to spend,
My life with you,
Come be with me.

Come share my smiles,
Come share my tears,
The good and bad,
Throughout the years,
Come be with me.

Come hold me tight,
Don't let me go,
I want you near,
I love you so,
Come be with me.

Magic Of The snow

See the snow as it comes down,
So soft and white and very pure,
Watch it settle on the ground,
That no longer can be seen.

It's really, really funny,
How the snow can make you change,
I feel like life has started me,
Toward a sweet and carefree way.

I love to watch the children,
As they laugh and as they play,
Oh! How happy they must be,
On such a snowy day.

Watch Out! Yells a youngster,
As you dodge a snowball fight,
There is no other beauty,
To match the snow at night.

Have you ever felt it?
The urge to be the one,
To run and laugh and play,
Again to be that young.

Snowmen, Angels watch them as they grow,
Trails from sleighs cutting through the snow.

Make Me No Promise

Make me no promise,
I ask you for none,
Just let me be with you,
As long as I can.

Fate! Do they call it?
I'm not sure what it be,
But burning desire,
Has been rooted in me.

I want to press to you,
'Til no closer we'll be,
To caress, hold and kiss you,
And you this to me.

Would you laugh if I told you,
These feelings are new?
The things that I read,
Are fantastically true.

Stars, bells, and whistles,
No none of those,
Just a warm fiery feeling,
From my head to my toes.

I want you to want me,
To grow to be one,
But make me no promise,
For I ask you for none.

Venus Fly Trap

Douglas went to Calisanti's,
Where he bought a plant,
That needs a lot of sunshine,
And feeds on flies and ants.

It needs a lot of water,
To keep it growing well,
It grows peculiar flowers,
But doesn't have a smell.

Its leaves lay there open,
They act like a tiny hand,
With its fingers spread so wide,
Waiting for something to land.

Its tiny hands close slowly,
Like two hands in prayer,
But we can see inside,
And his dinner is in there!

It's green and very different,
With leaves so long and thin,
The substance is very mossy,
That the "Venus Fly Trap" grows in.

Chrissy

So many years I've watched her play,
With her dollies and her toys,
Chasing others, playing tag,
Running, laughing, making noise.

But that must have been yesteryear,
Now a young lady's standing there,
No more lacey 'frilly dress,
Or little bows in her hair.

I felt a tug at my heart,
But only for a moment last,
Cause the beauty of my daughter,
Helped to set aside the past.

I wouldn't have it any other way,
Not playing with dollies and toys,
For now you see the time has come,
For her playthings to resemble boys.

My Son

Wee sweet child of my love,
From my body, heart and soul,
I give to you loving start,
The least to you I owe.

No other man could feel such pride,
I know your heart could burst,
When you go walking by his side,
In all things you are first.

I pray that Dad could see you son,
His name he'd know you bear,
His love I know, you would have won.
Just by being there.

My Grandma

Everyone needs a Grandma,
To spoil us some of the time,
Everyone loves their Grandma,
And I surely do love mine.

I love to hear her stories,
Of when I was so small,
And get to see my pictures,
She still hangs on the wall.

She bakes my favorite goodies,
And those things I love to eat,
I've tried to make the recipes,
But her talents hard to beat.

My Grandma is the greatest,
My Grandma is so fine,
Everyone loves their Grandma,
And I surely do love mine.

Angels Are Made In Heaven

Angels are made in heaven,
Dreams are made there too,
I must be blessed with goodness,
Because God gave me you.

I promised Him, I'd love you,
And keep you from life's harms,
To cherish and to hold you,
Safely in my arms.

I promised Him, I'd teach you,
What truth is all about,
And that it's quite alright,
To be sad and cry and shout.

But the thing I promised most,
Was my whole life to you,
So we can share it forever,
The way He'd want us to.

World Of Darkness

My world is dark around me,
Not a ray of sun is found,
I depend on other senses,
Like touch and smell and sound.

Please! Don't feel sorry for me,
That's not the thing to do,
Except that I am blind,
I'm just the same as you.

I can hear the birds that sing,
As they flutter through the air,
I can touch the gentle petals,
Of the flowers growing there.

I cannot see the colors,
That makes a rainbow grand,
But I hear the whisper of the wind,
And feel the grass growing on the ground.

I can tell you by your footsteps,
Feel your presence when you're near,
Identify you by your voice,
And I've been known to shed a tear.

Poor soul, how he must sufferer,
I hear some people say,
But they close their eyes to justice,
So I'd rather be this way.

Dear Lord

Dear Lord, it's time you take things over for me,
I've got too much to handle at this time,
The burdens of this life are full upon me,
And I find life's mountain just too high to climb.

It's not that I am shirking all my duties,
Or that I want to give them all to you,
It's just that I have finally reached my limit,
And I know this is the only thing to do.

I need my time to be a wife and mother,
These things are more important to me now,
And once my mind is clear from other worries,
I know everything will be all right somehow.

Amen.

Virginia

Virginia, how can I thank you?
For all you have done for me,
The days I need your humor,
And the time you've given free.

I really count me lucky,
I have found a friend in you,
Please promise you will let me know,
If there's anything I can do.

Goodness flows from you so easily,
The day won't come when you won't care,
For all of those around you,
For they know you're always there.

So thanks again, Virginia
For letting me be your friend,
And I hope neither miles nor years,
Will let this friendship end.

Send Me No Flowers

Send me no flowers,
Bad memories they bring,
Each time I receive them,
My heart feels a sting.

They give me no pleasure,
Or brighten my day,
And I fight the strong urge,
Just to throw them away.

I know that you love me,
And if you only knew,
That in sending me flowers,
You break me in two.

There are so many things,
That you could give, my dear,
So send me no flowers,
I do not want them near.

Someday it might be different,
And I'll even change my mind,
And the sadness that they hold,
Will be left somewhere behind.

Send me no flowers:
Bad memories they bring.

Hurting

Silently as I sit by,
As precious minutes flutter high,
I ask myself so tearfully,
Shall I give in or him to me?

Such silly things that should not toil,
Silly question who'll be loyal,
Is love so weak I cannot see?
What's hurting you is hurting me.

Through our kiss of love we know,
That with our love we both will grow,
Upon the land of loving peace,
And then the hurting words will cease.

Daddy, Are You there?

Daddy Do you hear me?
Daddy! Are you there?
Why don't you answer?
Is it that you don't hear?

I call every evening,
I ask in my prayer,
Daddy! Do you hear me?
Daddy! Are you there?

Why have you left me?
To live on my own,
To want and to miss you,
To go on alone?

Did you know what had happened?
Could you feel yourself go?
The love that I gave you,
Enough? My God no!

To go back to the start,
And try for once more,
I promise you, Daddy,
From my heart love will pour.

I'd never be bad,
Do exactly as you say,
Your best little girl,
I'd be every day.

Pride you would show,
With a smile on your face,
As you tell all your friends,
Of your girl all in lace.

What good is it now?
A promise won't do,
If only it would,
Would God give me back you?

New Friends

We moved to this fair town,
Not too awfully long ago,
We left behind our friends,
To make more as we'd go.

The sadness that we felt,
As the truck did pull away,
Would be replaced with joy,
At our new home far away.

The night of our goodbye party,
When we shed so many tears,
And the promise of writing letters,
And visits throughout the years.

And then when we are settled,
In to our new home town,
There's that dreadful fear of loneliness,
Until new friends we have found.

We faithfully write those letters,
Just as often as we plan,
But as the time does pass,
We write only when we can.

We never will forget you,
And we'll surely keep in touch,
But having found new interests,
It won't happen quite as much.

We love our new home town,
And the people here are great,
There's a reason we are here,
And I think they call it fate.

Jealousy

Jealousy! That awful green-eyed monster,
Lurks deep in everyone,
And he thrives upon those things,
That he has seen we've done.

When we're hurting he is happy,
Gets excited when we scream and yell,
And if he grows too big,
He will drive us all to Hell.

He enjoys the accusations,
That gives us cause to cry,
We can't beat that awful monster,
But we sure as hell can try.

Money – Money

Money! Money! Money!
That horrid, awful stuff,
But if we didn't have it,
Things surely would be tough.

Success

Will I ever be successful?
That is my dream you see,
Will I ever be successful?
If I am, I'll still be me.

Hungry Children

How can we sit there watching,
Or listening to their cries,
Seeing what hunger does to them,
Watch the suffering in their eyes.

"Times are hard for us" you say,
An extra buck is hard to find,
The price of a smoke or glass of booze,
Could food in ones tummy find.

Their suffering is so very great,
I think they'll surely die,
Searching for food in garbage piles,
Just so that they'll survive.

Little children don't you cry,
We will surely find a way
To help to fill those tummies,
So you'll live another day.

My Love Was Like A Rosebud

My love was like a rosebud,
Kissed by morning dew,
Its fragrance is so fresh,
Like the love I gave to you.

And like the tiny rosebud,
So delicate and small,
With just a little love and care,
The petals will not fall.

But pluck it from its stem,
You could almost hear it cry,
It's as if that tiny rosebud,
Knows that it will die.

My love was once that easy,
To crush, to wither and kill,
But you put a fence around me,
And here I'm growing still.

But some of my tiny petals,
Are a little worse for wear,
My stem leans over slightly,
And thorns are growing there.

I no longer sway so freely,
In the gentle summer breeze,
All my petals now are open,
And there are holes now in my leaves.

But unlike that tiny rosebud,
I had someone to care,
Although I'm worn and tattered,
I know he's always there.

Daydreaming

Sometimes, I catch myself daydreaming,
As my thoughts take me back home,
To the wide open spaces,
And the people I've once known.

I remember the flowing river,
Where I could of sat all day,
To feel the peace around me,
And to watch the waters play.

I still see the big old bridge,
Where I stood to watch the view,
And every time I stood there,
I was pleased with something new.

I still can feel the country air,
Blowing soft and smelling sweet,
Playfully swaying the grass and trees,
And buttercups at my feet.

Not a worry in this whole world,
Did I have while I was there,
It's as if that flowing river,
And I had dreams to share.

Someday, I hope that I can go,
Back to my old home town,
To the easy country living,
And the peace that I once found.

Dear Friend

It has been quite a while,
Since I've sat and wrote to you,
Every time I think of it,
I've got something else to do.

It's not that I've forgotten,
Or ran out of things to say,
It's just when I'm not busy,
Other things get in the way.

But now I've found a minute,
To ask you how you are,
How is your man and family?
I wish you didn't live so far.

And as I write this letter,
Memories flood my head,
Of how we chummed together,
Just like sisters, so they said.

And when we needed someone,
Each of us was always there,
To give a smile or wipe a tear,
And to show someone would care.

We shared our many secrets,
No one else was to know,
Where ever one of us had gone,
The other would also go.

But now we're grown and married,
And have gone our separate ways,
But best friends we'll always be
Until our dying days.

Because He's Part of Me

It's hard to live with someone,
When he's going through such pain,
And when you think all's well,
It starts all over again.

When he hurts, I do feel for him,
It is 'easy to do you see,
I know him, oh so well,
Because he's part of me.

A silent prayer I offer,
To the greatest power above,
I will do all that you ask,
But help the man I love.

Take the burdens from him,
Help to ease his mind,
Give him the strength he needs,
And teach me to be kind.

Someone Sits Here

Someone sits here waiting,
For the telephone to ring,
To hear your voice again,
And the feeling it does bring.

Someone sits here listening,
To every single sound,
Hoping that the next one,
Means you have come around.

Someone sits here wishing,
That you are on your way,
To tell how you do care,
And will be here to stay.

Someone sits here smiling,
As thoughts go through one's head,
Remembering the special things,
That we once did and said.

Someone sits here crying,
Cause you forgot to call,
You didn't try to come around,
You mustn't care at all.

Someone sits here broken-hearted,
But wait! What do I hear?
The phone: Oh yes! Hello, hello!
It's nice to hear you dear.

Someone sits here bursting,
With happiness and glee:
Cause that special someone,
Will soon be here with me.

Telltales of A Broken Heart

Yesterday I was smiling,
Heard music in my head
I know my eyes were shining,
Now tears are there instead.

How could I know about her?
Or that he'd go away,
When he said 'I love you'
I never thought it'd end this way.

I no longer wear a smile,
Or hear music in my head,
And if my eyes are shining,
It's because of tears instead.

I don't care if the sun ain't shining,
It means not a thing to me,
My heart has just been broken,
It can't be mended, don't you see.

Telltales of a broken heart,
Are what you left for me.

"Share a Smile"

Listen, can you hear it?
The laughter that eases pain,
Feel it, swirl around you,
The warmth of caring once again.

Reach out, and we will guide you,
Into our special world of fun,
Share it, for it's contagious,
It can be had by everyone.

Find it, but do not keep it,
Pass it on to all you know,
What is it? It's "Share a Smile",
Plant the seed and watch it grow.

"Angels Touch"

The touch of an Angel, upon my hair,
The feeling of serenity everywhere.
The sound of my Angel as she sings,
The fluttering softness of her wings.

This is the gift that God does send,
He sends it all in the form of a friend.
I know for a fact that this is true.
For you, are my friend, and He sent me you.

So, precious Angel, I want you to see
Without your friendship, I would not be.
My life would be different, for that I am sure,
And days filled with pain I could not endure.

Thank you my Angel, God's gift from above.
I in return will pass on that love.
I give it freely just as you give it to me.
Your Angel, I pray that someday I'll be.

Shared Years

Just today I was thinking,
Of the last married years,
And how we worked together,
Sharing laughter, hope, and fears.

There were times if things got harder,
I was sure we'd fall apart,
But we suffered through it all,
And it even made us smart.

It's funny what we remember,
And what we'll forget too,
The right things overshadow,
The wrong things we do.

Christine, Doug, and Albert,
Better we could not have done,
A lovely blue eyed daughter,
And two very handsome sons.

You've brought me so much pleasure,
In the many years we've shared,
And you've overlooked my many faults,
Proving that you cared.

We've never been as happy,
As we are today,
And if our hardships over,
It will always be this way.

It hurts to think about it,
That we will go astray,
So we will go on loving,
So it will never be that way.

Silent Love

Isn't life funny?
Dreams do come true,
I looked up from my table,
And there I found you.

I knew at a moment,
Together we'd be,
For when our eyes met,
You smiled at me.

You walked to my table,
And without even a word,
Sat down beside me,
Not a sound could be heard.

You reached over to me,
Taking hold of my hand,
And gave me a look,
We'd both understand.

Nothing was said,
Nor need it be,
Cause I love you,
And I knew you loved me.

Buffy &Peanuts

Everyone needs someone waiting,
When our daily work is through,
But God has chosen me special,
Cause he has given me two.

Two hearts so very full of love,
Just waiting at the door,
For me to come on home,
Each day I love them more.

They've got the biggest brown eyes,
That cheers my saddest day,
I feel so warm inside,
When they turn and look my way.

Baffle, soft, small, and curly,
Has a place upon my chair
And Peanuts curled up beside me,
Is also laying there.

The love we share is precious,
I love them, oh so much,
There isn't any doubt they know,
They can tell it by my touch.

Jimmy, I know you're smiling,
Watching me with these dears,
Buffy and Peanuts, a part of my life,
That overpowers all my fears.

Momma

Momma! Can't you see I'm crying?
Won't you extend a loving hand,
Or lend a comforting shoulder,
Or hug me where I stand?

I crave for your motherly powers,
To wash away all sadness and pain,
To put your love around me,
Like an umbrella protects from rain.

Momma, do I love you?
I really cannot say,
Whenever I tried to show you,
You only walked away.

I'm sorry things aren't all rosy,
Or happiness, all peaches and cream,
But no one promised it simple,
And things can't be as hard as they seem.

So Momma: See why I'm crying,
Please, extend a loving hand,
Lend a comforting shoulder,
And hug me where I stand.

Give me a chance to love you,
And I will try to understand.

I'm Hurting

Has there ever been a time when you hurt so bad and crying seemed the only thing to do?
When your heart felt like it was breaking and your stomach tied in knots; well, I am, and
I'm not sure what I should do.

Do I pretend what I see isn't so?
Do I hope and I pray he won't want to go?
Do I close my eyes, pretend I don't see,
He's looking my way, but not seeing me.

So many years I've spent by his side
Now all my fears from him I must hide
He says that he loves me but if that's true,
Why does he spend so much, time with you?
She's only a friend; a friend's all she'll be,
We've nothing in common; she means nothing to me,
These are the words he revealingly said,
Then why am I crying: lying here on my bed?

I know I am foolish to lay here and cry,
But you're breaking my heart, and you do know why,
So, if you do love me as much as you say,
Take me instead, don't call on her today.

Nature And 1

Here I am on top this hill,
The wind blowing through my hair,
Flowers blooming all around,
God's beauty everywhere.

I feel the sun upon my face,
The soft grass beneath my feet,
Watch the grace of birds fly by,
Toward a velvet blue retreat.

White fluffy clouds dot the sky,
Making my imagination soar,
Building castles ships or things,
I can open any door.

The air so fresh, sweet and mild,
Blowing its fragrances around,
Gathering them as it goes along,
Kissing flowers, trees, and ground.

The silence is truly golden,
Only nature can be heard,
The chirping of the cricket,
And the singing of the bird.

Alone, I'm not, I assure you!
How can this be, you say?
All of God's glorious beauty,
Has kept me company today.

Lost Friendships

What ever happened to that friend,
I had so long ago?
Sharing dreams and sharing tears,
Together fighting foe.

I often think about that friend,
Wherever she might be,
I often wonder how frequently,
My friend will think of me.

Time does pass and life must change,
We all must go our way,
And as I watch my children,
I'd remember how we'd play.

It really, is so very sad,
What miles and years have done,
They have taken the best of friendships,
And erased them one by one.

What ever happened to that friend,
I loved and cared for so?
She is only just a memory,
Of a life so long ago.

Other books written and published by Christine Hannon are:

A Hairdresser's Diary
A Hairdresser's Diary: Scissors Retired
Say it With a Poem
Flabbermouth Moments
A Cut Above Discrimination

All are available on Amazon, LULU, Smashwords, Kobo. Kindle IBooks and many other places in many different formats. They are available in either softcover or e book or both formats.

Stay tuned there are two more in the making at the time of this publishing.

www.ahairdressersdiary.com